THE
ANTI
RACIST
TEACHER

READING INSTRUCTION
WORKBOOK

Second Edition

LORENA GERMÁN

Executive Director: Roberto Germán
Cover and text designs, typesetting: Monica Ann Cohen
Permissions: Renee Nicholls
Editing: Tanya Manning-Yarde, Lois Barker

For more information regarding permission, please write to Multicultural Classroom, PO Box 340744, Tampa, FL 33694.

To the girl
who was still bold,
still intelligent,
and still ambitious
when her teachers
tried to stop her.
Look at you.

THE ANTIRACIST TEACHER: READING INSTRUCTION WORKBOOK EXTENDS AN OPEN INVITATION FOR READING TEACHERS TO DO INTROSPECTIVE WORK. ITS PURPOSE IS COMMUNITY CREATION. PROGRESS AND LIBERATION WON'T HAPPEN IN ISOLATION. THE MOVEMENT

TOWARD RACIAL JUSTICE AND EQUITY WILL ONLY HAPPEN TOGETHER. THANK YOU FOR JOINING THIS COMMUNITY. THANK YOU FOR CONSIDERING THIS WORKBOOK AS A COMPASS.

LET'S DIG IN.

THERE'S SO MUCH WORK TO DO.

CONTENTS

FOREWORD

THE ANTIRACIST TEACHER: READING INSTRUCTION WORKBOOK
is a blueprint, a guide, a call to action. It's your best teaching friend, the one who will hold you accountable to your community and yourself. I'm so honored to know Lorena Germán; to call her my friend, to know she will always hold me accountable to our community, and be there to dream of a better, more just world.

I've admired (and been SO inspired by) Lorena's work since I first attended a writing workshop she and Roberto (of Multicultural Classroom) shared with the Montessori community in 2018. Carrying her sleeping newborn in her arms, Lorena pushed us to be creative, introspective, culturally critical, and expansive.

I continually return to Lorena and her work because everything she offers to us is absolutely necessary and foundational. We can no longer make excuses when it comes to enacting positive antiracist change within ourselves and our communities, because Lorena provides us with the framework. And, with this updated edition, we get to dive even deeper into ensuring that we, the readers, understand what the traits of the prevailing dominant culture are. Lorena guides us through reflections to support learning and growth and shares even more knowledge through her research, footnotes, and guidance. This small book is packed with everything we need to become better teachers and humans. Lorena offers us an act of love for liberation with the addition of a corresponding course that encourages us all to thoughtfully apply our new knowledge in our own classrooms and learning spaces.

Foreword by Tiffany Jewell
#1 New York Times Bestselling Author of *This Book is Antiracist*

ACKNOWLEDGMENTS

THE ANTIRACIST TEACHER: READING INSTRUCTION WORKBOOK wouldn't have been possible without the support of a whole crew of dedicated, loving, and hardworking people. My husband, Roberto, was instrumental in making it possible for me to complete this work for all of you. My sister, Francesca, was crucial in coaching me through the production of it all. My cousin Wanda designed the original cover, and now Monica Cohen has helped with this new edition. I'm eternally grateful. My friend editors: Jineyda, Dan, Katie, Sarah, and Julia gave insight and suggested improvements. This second edition also had two editors and I want to thank them both for their time and intentional readings. Thank you, Tanya and Lois for giving this book your attention.

I'm so excited for us and the work we have ahead. I hope that this workbook is helpful to you. I hope that these readings and these questions help us all to do better for the sake of our future. My prayer is that this workbook will sustain the fire in our bellies.

I want us to pay attention to all the details and know that our impact in the classroom is felt so we need to make it count. Does our impact function to promote racial justice and liberation? Does your work in the classroom cause young people to value lives and not believe in killing? Does your teaching approach dismantle the hurt and pain historically caused by schooling?

These are big questions and an important process. I'm honored we are on this journey together.

The hands of White Supremacy have been choking us—killing Black and Brown people in this nation. They're murdering us, imprisoning us, failing us, pushing us out, and more. Those hands have created the poison that is rotting White America. Racism is hurting us all. I hope that this work really does help liberate us from White Supremacy.

¡Pa'lante en la lucha!

WELCOME!

WHAT A TRIP THIS BOOK HAS TAKEN ALL AROUND THE world. It's been exciting and encouraging to watch. This second edition aims to expand some of the ideas and keep alive the energy toward antiracist teaching and living. The call to action is still the same: becoming antiracist through research, reflection, and practice.

Whether you've been digging in this work before, or this is your first step, welcome. Angela Davis tells us that, "In a racist society, it's not enough to be non-racist, we must be anti-racist." For some of us antiracism means probing deep within ourselves to find the ways that we've internalized the racism cloaked over us and used to oppress us. For some, it means analyzing how your behavior is steeped in White Supremacy and upholding the systems your ancestors designed. Regardless of how you walk into the work, we know there is work to do.

There are some minor changes throughout this second edition. First, you'll notice that there are footnotes here and there. I kept the citations in my format as a way to make sure the research and readings are still accessible. Also, since when is MLA or APA the "only" way to prove credibility?! And you'll notice I've expanded different sections and added more context. I decided to do this based on the professional development sessions I've led and book clubs I've been a part of related to this book, and the consistent questions I get. Now, let's get back to it.

In 2019, Learning for Justice (a project of the Southern Poverty Law Center) published the "Hate at School Report." The findings of the report are astounding and painful to read. The results are part of the impetus for this workbook and the work we should be committed to. Did you know that in 2017 about 35% of students reported being worried and anxious about hate and bias at school? Did you know that when teachers discriminate against students those students question their academic abilities and belonging at school? Did you know that racial and ethnic hate and bias are often experienced in the form of "slurs and racist iconography"? Did you know that over 60% of hate and bias incidents happen at the middle and high school level and that over 30% of those incidents occur in the classroom? I didn't.

This second edition was written in February of 2023, four years after the first edition. Our society hasn't evolved into antiracism as it should have. Last month we saw the murder of Tyre Nichols at the hands of police. Just last night, a mass shooter attacked Michigan State University. Black Lives Matter movements are still relevant and necessary, but support for that movement has declined since the summer of 2020.[1] As expected, teens are more likely to support the movement vs. adults.[2] This is where we educators come in because we can be critical in exposing young people to the set of facts and truth necessary to cultivate new visions for our lives. We are positioned to do powerful work in the shaping of our nation. It's always been this way, but our predecessors didn't use that power for antiracism. Not only is a different future possible, but we are in a position to make it happen. What a privilege!

How much better off would young people be if the adults in their lives were antiracist? And once we know we're antiracist, we have to be able to answer the question: What do you stand for? If you're against racism, then what are you for? This isn't a trick question. Indeed, it is so important for us to be hope-filled and forward-looking when it comes to doing antiracism work. We are

1. "Support for Black Lives Matter Surged Last Year. Did It Last?" was a strong opinion essay published by Jennifer Chudy & Hakeem Jefferson via the New York Times in 2021.

2. Pew Research Center published this article in June of 2022 by Kiley Hurst entitled, "U.S. teens are more likely than adults to support the Black Lives Matter movement."

literally trying to envision and see a future that we've never seen before. We must dream. We must imagine a new way of being.

I find that when we talk about antiracism, we are rarely including colonialism as part of the root of the problem. Racism began when Europeans had the idea that they could travel to another land, take it, and dispossess (then murder) the people of that land. Therefore, anti-Indigenous colonialism must be a central part of the conversation and effort of antiracism. We also cannot ignore the intersectionality of the way racism functions. Gender, class, ability, religion, citizenship status, sexuality, and more, complicate our experiences in this interdisciplinary project called White Supremacy. In my growth, I've learned that when I talk about antiracism I mean: racial equity, racial justice, redistribution of power, reparations, and rebuilding. All of the institutions and systems in this country need to be rebuilt. Until then, we inspect and correct.

I hope that as educators we believe in the potential and power of the young people sitting in front of us. That's how we ended up in this work, right? We believe that they really are the ones that will either change this country or maintain the current racist status quo. There are many factors playing a role in what they'll become, and educators are one of them. We are one of those factors and have the power to inspire them to see differently and act boldly. We cannot underestimate our impact as teachers.

There are so many aspects to teaching literature. So much of what we do comes from a pre-existing structure and system that we were educated in; ways we inherited. There are actions we take and beliefs we hold as literature instructors that we didn't necessarily choose for ourselves. There were, and continue to be, so many practices I'm revisiting and undoing myself. I'm not above this work. My sleeves are up and I'm digging in, too.

And so, *The Antiracist Teacher: Reading Instruction Workbook* is for everybody. We all have to do this work.

I want Latines, African Americans, Black Americans, Asians, Asian Americans, and Indigenous people of this land to reconsider and evaluate themselves using this workbook. Whose values are we holding onto tightly and how are those values impacting young people? I was thinking of you as I worked on this. I did this because I love you; because I love us. White folks, we need you, too. As descendants of colonizers, you have so much undoing to take on. The work before you is critical and essential. This is not about shame. Take that pain and turn it into a fierce love for justice and righteousness.

WHAT YOU'LL FIND IN THIS BOOK:

The book is structured in sections with each containing quotes, images, or paraphrased bullet points from books that invite us into a nuanced exploration of race(ism). I know teachers are busy and it can be really difficult to read an entire book, especially an academically dense one during the school year. What I've done is taken some of the most salient points from those books and put them into this one. Then, paired them with opportunities for reflection and application. In the first section, "An Exploration of Traits of White Supremacy Culture in Reading Instruction," I offer a framework for seeing this culture in our classrooms. I present practical steps for dismantling white supremacist ways in reading instruction.

Next, in the "*Culturally Sustaining Pedagogy* Reflection Exercise " section, I dig into the contents of the book by Dr. Paris and Dr. Alim and include personal reflection opportunities focused on an inclusive teaching approach.

Then, in the "'Suspending Damage' Reflection Exercise" section, I include some more reflection including excerpts from Eve Tuck's powerful letter.

We transition to the one and only Toni Morrison by focusing on her work in *Playing in the Dark*. We think about race and the imagination in reading instruction.

Next, Claudia Rankine's work in *Citizen* grants us an opportunity for personal reflection.

And to wrap up the reflection portion, we end with a concept from Dr. Ibram X. Kendi's *How to Be An Antiracist.* His book leads you to think about antiracist ideology and I apply it to reading instruction. Lastly, I present a series of practical strategies and tips for classroom antiracist practices.

The purpose of *The Antiracist Teacher: Reading Instruction Workbook* is for reading teachers to have a resource we can turn to in order to do necessary introspective antiracist work. Second, its purpose is to create a community for us. Progress and liberation won't happen in isolation. The movement toward racial justice and equity will only happen in community. Thank you for joining this community. Thank you for considering this workbook in your journey. Let's dig in.

There's so much work to do.

BEFORE WE BEGIN . . .

I'M GOING TO BE USING TERMS THROUGHOUT THIS WORKBOOK that may be new to you. I think the language we use is critical in what we communicate and how our intentions are received. There are so many terms we use in conversations about race and racism and while we're using the same words, people might easily be meaning different things. For example, many people have different definitions of what racism is. Some see it as individual acts based in racism and others see it as a systemic problem, going beyond the individual interaction. And while this word has an actual definition, people don't always use it accordingly. This misuse of language leads to miscommunication and furthers tension. Therefore, I want to take the time to define the terms I'm using, so we're on the same page.

White gaze: This term denotes the White-centered/Eurocentric vision that dominates White American society. In the case of this workbook, I am talking about the presence of white-centered literature and texts. It is a world-view where the audience is assumed to be white, where plots and lives are for white people to understand and consume.

People of the Global Majority/People of Color (PoGM/PoC): This is a term I use to refer to who we all call People of Color. I use that term so that we can keep in mind the truth that we are a global majority. It also shifts the dynamic of thinking that we are "minorities," in other words, less than.

White Supremacy: This is the belief at the root of our system which upholds that Whiteness/White race as superior to other ways of being and existing. It is at the foundation of all institutions in this country. This term is not about one individual or skin color, but about an institution.

Pedagogy(ies): Pedagogy, by definition, is the craft of teaching. Scholars often use this term to encompass praxis, or practice of teaching. This is why we can use it in the plural, because it's really a set of crafts and practices.

— • —

As we begin, I want to start with a framework to shape our understanding of White Supremacy culture. As stated, while we use the same words, at times, we don't always mean the same ideas. As a result, in this first section we are exploring the traits of a White Supremacy culture.

This is a controversial set of ideas because Whiteness, the institution, doesn't want to acknowledge itself. If we see the monster; if we see the problem, we can address it, right? As such, the myth is that silence is more comfortable. If we think of our society, though, racism is a disease that is killing us all. We must expose it and make its bones bare so we can destroy it.

When I speak of White Supremacy culture, what I mean is the beliefs, the ideas, the values, that surround the actions we would normally point to as "racist." These actions begin as ideas. They begin as sentiments that go unchecked, and at some point, the individual feels welcomed to take actions based on those beliefs. This is culture.

Consider this comparison: Students at School X often stand in the hallway in between class and tease one another based on appearances. While this is simply teasing, and not outright bullying, students aren't always reprimanded and consequences for these behaviors aren't clear or consistently executed. No one really likes this reality, but it continues. Obviously, students have these thoughts and feel comfortable enough, welcomed even, to express their ideas by taking these mocking actions in the hallway. This is now the culture at this school.

Similarly, White Supremacy is a culture and it is the foundation of our society. If you feel uncomfortable as you read this and want to disassociate yourself from this culture, good. We should all feel that way. We should all hate White Supremacy culture. But in order for us to make sure we're not participating in it and instead are actively working against it, we must itemize it and learn to see it. We will be using the work of Tema Okun as a framework to develop a new lens with which to see the world around us. These new glasses will help us do both external and internal reflection. Are you ready to dive in?

"WHITE SUPREMACY CULTURE IS A DEVASTATING FORCE IN ALL OUR LIVES, USED BY RULING CLASS POWER BROKERS TO MAINTAIN VAST AND VIOLENT STRUCTURAL INEQUALITY."
— TEMA OKUN

AN EXPLORATION OF THE TRAITS OF WHITE SUPREMACY CULTURE IN READING INSTRUCTION

TEMA OKUN, A WHITE WOMAN, SPENT SOME TIME, ALONG WITH Kenneth Jones and other researchers observing and evaluating what we call white culture. Together, they developed a list of traits that define White Supremacy culture originally published in 1999.[3] It's interesting to read them because as an insider to White culture, she has extensive knowledge and can describe how these traits show up in organizations.

Considering how our identities play a role in meaning making when encountering texts (Ebarvia 2023),[4] prioritizing identity in the process is crucial to doing comprehensive and deeply meaningful work with students. Okun's work grants us a framework, specific to race, to analyze how racism is enacted during reading instruction in U.S. classrooms. I want to invite us to think about how these traits are present in our classrooms and schools. Culture is powerful because it shapes our entire life. Yet, it can be difficult to pin down. Below is a list of the traits Tema Okun (and

---

3. You can learn more by visiting Tema Okun's website called white-supremacyculture.info. It's visually pleasing because she's included artwork and so much more.
4. Tricia Ebarvia published *Get Free: Antibias Literacy Instruction for Stronger Readers, Writers, and Thinkers* in 2023 and she breaks down the intertwined relationship between literacy, identity, and bias.

others) identified:

1. Perfectionism
2. Sense of urgency
3. Defensiveness
4. Quantity over quality
5. Worship of the written word
6. Paternalism
7. Either/or thinking
8. Power hoarding
9. Fear of open conflict
10. Individualism
11. Progress is bigger, more
12. Objectivity
13. Right to comfort

What I appreciate about her work is that she focuses on how all of this builds a culture. It's not about an individual, but a collective. While all of these could be expanded upon to analyze reading instruction, I have selected seven I wanted us to focus on. I have adapted their definitions and explanations in order to think about them through the lens of reading instruction.

One of the biggest challenges of accepting the truth of these traits is how we might see them as social norms because "this is how it's always been." We might even want to reject them as racialized, because they seem so "universal." But we must be self-critical and openly evaluate these ideas. because They promote White Supremacy thinking. They promote the violent harm that is at the foundation of our country.

I hope we can agree that most early colonizers were racists. Therefore, we can agree that their shared values and beliefs were also racist. Behavior can mostly be attributed to values. The values of these colonizers are directly connected to the traits outlined by Okun. Figure 1 is a graphic that makes direct connections between the actions of early colonizers and the traits of White Supremacy

Figure 1: The Average Colonizer

Striving for more land and conquering of people groups (power hoarding)

Concerned about achieving more and fast (sense of urgency)

Ready for war because of perceived fears and attacks (defensiveness)

Destroys the words and cultures of Indigenous people because he perceives them to be lesser than (power hoarding & worship of the written word)

Determines what's best for the new conquered people and in some cases, believes he owns them (paternalism)

One leader, one source of power (individualism)

Obtaining land, food, and resources at the expense of others (right to comfort)

And more...

culture.

Early colonizers wanted more land and in order to acquire that land, they had to conquer the people that inhabited it. This is an example of power hoarding. They wanted power. They wanted the power of land ownership, the power of wealth, and of control. They were concerned about achieving these acquisitions, and others, fast. They wanted to urgently move the project of colonization forward. This is an example of having a sense of urgency as outlined by Okun. These colonizers were constantly at war, starting wars, and engaging in deadly battles with the people of this land because of perceived and conjured fears and attacks. They believed to be under fire and to be themselves targets of evil, whilst being the attackers and promoting evil actions on human beings. Okun explains how the power of the written word is about valuing that form of communication and literacy over all others and early colonizers across the Americas would burn their cultural artifacts, including their historical documents.

Through this destruction, they would oppress the people they had met and believed they owned them. This paternalistic behavior led them to believe they actually knew what was best for them. The early colonizers' leadership structure was one we continue to follow today: one ruler with one source of power. Yes, today we have checks and balances and there are many people who participate in the decision-making process of this country, but in the end, we still function as a society with one leader at the helm. This individualistic pattern of leadership and thinking can be seen in the actions and ways of early colonizers. Lastly, Okun points out how the perceived right to comfort is a central trait of White Supremacy culture and we see that performed by early colonizers. Their believed right to comfort allowed them to steal land, food, resources, and rights at the expense of others for their personal benefit.

Their behaviors can be attributed to their values, and those values are directly connected to the traits listed above. In Figure 1, I analyze an early colonizer by making direct connections between these traits and his behaviors.

The early colonizers settled and their descendants designed the institutions that continue to be in our society today. Their beliefs and values were passed on as culture and as morality. These institutions, education included, were built on these values. This is not a theory or a belief of mine. This is simply history. Therefore, we have to think about who they were, how they were, and how we might see their footprint in our society today.

My point is that the aspects of our culture that we think are common sense and good practice, are purely subjective and based on our context. They also often stem from White Supremacy culture. Okun explains that, "Because we all live in a White Supremacy culture, these characteristics show up in the attitudes and behaviors of all of us—People of Color and White people. Therefore, these attitudes and behaviors can show up in any group or organization, whether it is white-led, or predominantly white, or People of Color-led, or predominantly People of Color." (whitesupremacyculture.info) Similarly for us, these beliefs are embedded in our educational system and pedagogical practices. However, if we don't know what these traits are, there is no way for us to identify them. That is why this workbook is here. I want to walk you through the journey of exploring these traits, identifying them at large, and then identifying them in your own practice. What we are doing next is walking through the seven traits I selected and understanding what they are, how they might show up, and strategies that can counter them.

Trait: *Perfectionism*

The pursuit of perfection can take on racist undertones, especially when the goals and standards of perfection are racialized. This means that the standards and goals of success are attributed to one group but are something to strive toward for other groups, and the distinguishing factor is race. This means that perfection is owned by some, while remaining an unattainable goal for others. Consider which people groups are commonly associated with perfect hair, perfect bodies, perfect communities, and so on. Here are some ways to think of perfectionism in classrooms:

- Little appreciation or positive feedback is exchanged among students for the efforts and achievements of their peers.
- Typically, expressing appreciation is usually directed to students who are already regarded as strong or fast reader.
- It is more common to criticize someone's reading errors or their inadequacy as readers.
- A classroom culture where students gossip about others' reading skills or abilities.
- Reading errors are perceived as personal (they reflect poorly on the person making them) rather than being

seen for what they are: mistakes.
- Reading instruction that focuses on what's wrong and leaves students with little ability to identify, name, and appreciate what's right.

A student exposed to this pedagogical approach may internalize these ideas of perfectionism concerning their reading identity, exhibiting the following reading attitudes:

- They self-identify as perfectionists and view this as a positive trait while failing to appreciate their own reading progress.
- They frequently often point out their failures and the shortcomings of their peers.
- They hyperfocus on their inadequacies shortcomings about in reading, reading completion, and comprehension.

Ways to dismantle perfectionism in reading instruction:

- Create a reading culture of appreciation where students' skills and abilities are celebrated.
- Help students understand that mistakes are expected and are opportunities for growth.
- See mistakes as separate from the person, not as a defining trait.
- Provide positive feedback before feedback identifying areas of growth and truly.
- Celebrate students with substantive observations
- Openly talk about reading discomfort and demystifying debunk fears.

Here are sentence starters designed to encourage open discussion with students about their reading discomforts & demystifying fears.

- Something that makes me uncomfortable when I'm

reading is . . .
- A discomfort I have when reading aloud is . . .
- I'm afraid to . . . when reading because . . .
- Reading causes me to feel . . .

Trait: *Sense of Urgency*

A sense of urgency can perpetuate racist systems when it is used against people groups to demand more of them in a dehumanizing way, among other explanations. Think of the ways Black and Brown people have historically been urged to work until death, forced to sacrifice their peace and humanity for the comfort of others, or made to perform and give at the expense of their own needs. This sense of urgency manifests in a myriad of ways. Below you'll see how it can be present in classrooms:

- There is a persistent sense of urgency that hinders the ability to take the necessary time to involve others in the reading process or consider the various levels or speed of reading.
- The class engages in whole class reading experiences where the expectation is for reading to be fast and students are not offered the opportunity to read at their own pace.
- The sense of urgency doesn't allow the teacher to engage students in discussion about nuanced, difficult topics because they must prioritize "test-taking" skills. For example, novels and texts are read quickly in order to expedite the work that must be completed. This transforms the act or reading into a task to complete vs. reading to empathize, grow, and learn.

A student in this classroom exposed to this type of reading instruction may internalize a sense of urgency regarding their reading identity, exhibiting the following reading attitudes:

- Feeling rushed to complete work because completion is

Figure 2: Exploring Reader Identities

EXPLORING READER IDENTITIES		
Books that you have read & enjoy reading:	What people say about you as a reader:	I'm the kind of writer who...
I read because . . .	What people say about you as a writer:	I write because . . .

more important than quality
- Taking pride in the speed in which they submit their work
- Feeling frustrated when they fail to meet goals by a predetermined deadline and then react negatively to mistakes (as mentioned in perfectionism).

Ways to dismantle a sense of urgency in reading instruction include:

- Recognize that reading, comprehension, and analysis take time and are a cyclical process, not bound by an exam.
- Invest time discussing students' reader identities and emotions related to reading.
- Be transparent with students about the time constraints you do have and engage in an open dialogue about achievable goals.

Figure 2 is a chart I've used before with students to help them explore their reader identities and reading-related emotions. I've used this at the start of the school year to get to know them personally and as readers. Students have often found this to be a positive questionnaire since they've rarely been asked about their reader identities. These can also be a multi-day lesson by having students do one prompt a day in an index card.

Trait: *Defensiveness*

Feeling defensive is a very human emotion, but there's another level of defensiveness that is pernicious in the context of racism. This defensiveness is afraid and uncomfortable talking about race, dealing with racial confrontation, facing truth, identifying racist structures, and engaging in self work toward progress. This defensiveness is stimulated when we are in a tense moment and feel as though we are under attack, but we might not actually be. There is a difference between accountability and an attack. The main problem with this defensiveness is that it functions as an obstacle and prohibits growth. In the classroom, it can look like:

- Highly monitoring the act of reading with much energy spent following the "reading rules" rather than promoting a love of reading and student choice
- Responding to new or challenging ideas, authors, genres, and/or forms with defensiveness, making it very difficult to make suggestions that promote diversity
- Spending energy defending against charges of racism instead of examining how racism is actually happening
- Perceiving calls for change as personal attacks.

A student in this classroom exposed to this type of reading instruction may internalize defensiveness regarding their reading identity. They may exhibiting the following reading attitudes:

- Believing that they cannot make suggestions for new titles or share interests in voices other than the ones represented in the teachers' curriculum
- Seeing an attack on "classical" texts as personal attacks and negative critiques without considering the value in exercising differing points of view.

Ways to dismantle defensiveness in reading instruction:

- Understanding that defensiveness is connected to fear of losing power
- Making space for yourself and for your students to consider books (and all forms of text) outside of what is considered the literary canon
- Naming defensiveness as a problem when it is one and work on your own defensiveness
- Discussing with students in a conversation about how defensiveness of the canon has allowed for marginalized voices to be historically excluded from classrooms.

Addressing defensiveness can take place in a variety of ways. I often do this through 1-1 conversations with students. I use questions such as the ones below:

- "Are you feeling defensive? That's what it looks like to me. If so, why do you think that is?"
- "Are you noticing your defensiveness right now? What is making you feel this way and why do you think that is?"
- "Why is this bringing up discomfort for you and what about moving forward is hard?"
- "How can I support you to tackle the defensiveness you're feeling right now?"

Trait: *Quantity Over Quality*

To understand our obsession with quantity over quality, just look at how success is often measured by how much you have instead of how good you are. For example, someone who has many companies, a lot of money, and many properties is considered more successful than someone who is an expert in their field. This is unique to us; unique to the United States. Lives matter less than property here.

Consider the racial protests we saw in 2020 and the concern shared by many for the potential losses to local properties and small businesses. Remember the example of the early colonizer we began this workbook with. He has much wealth, land, and slaves. This makes him successful, in spite of the fact that he is an enslaver. We value quantity over depth. We value numerous acquaintances over one close best friend.

This trait can manifest in classrooms in some of the following ways:

- Reading instruction prioritizes producing measurable goals.
- Tasks that can be measured are more highly valued than tasks that cannot.

- There is little to no value attached to process; if it can't be measured, it is deemed without value.
- The quantity of books is prioritized over the types of books students are reading and their meaningfulness.

A student in this classroom receiving this type of instruction may internalize a sense of quantity over quality in terms of their reading identity. They may exhibit the following reading attitudes:

- They prioritize the number of pages and books they've read over comprehension.
- They emphasize reading speed, which is another example of a sense of urgency.

Ways to dismantle a sense of urgency in reading instruction include the following:

- Create space for students to value process, slowing down, and finding meaning instead of valuing the number of pages or books completed.
- Take breaks in the unit to respond to needs and to process reading the book(s) with students.

Below are some sentence starters you can use to pause and process the reading with students:

- "How is this reading making you feel?"
- "Is the text bringing up big feelings about ? Why or why not?"
- "How might this text be trying to dig into our lives and our past histories?"
- "I'm feeling _____. Is anyone else having similar feelings or thoughts?"

Trait: *Worship of the Written Word*

It is very important to clarify that while this phrase hints at Christianity and the Bible, that is not specifically what this is about. In our nation, we have a tendency to prioritize and respect the written alphabet over any other form of literacy. Think about our laws: if something is said, it doesn't count as much as if it were written. If something is signed, it's now a contract and our humanity means nothing in its presence.

On its own, this isn't necessarily racist, but to understand colonization is to understand how it was also a war in the field of language. Treaties were weaponized against Indigenous people demonstrating how those in power exploited written word policies. Literacy tests, initially designed to suppress African American voting rights, were doubly insidious as literacy had been forbidden for them for decades.

The over-valuing of the written alphabet, or the worship of the written word, can show up in classrooms in the following ways:

- Non- "traditional" books in print don't count as reading
- Alternate forms of reading and texts are not valued or welcomed.
- Teachers predominantly commend students who can read quickly and those who prefer include the traditional "classical texts."
- Only a specific type of language is esteemed and permitted to exist in the classroom.
- The curriculum includes only books using Dominant American English as well as British English, diminishing and critiquing any book containing any other form of English.

A student exposed to this pedagogical approach may internalize a reverence for the written word in terms of their reading identity. They may exhibit the following reading attitudes:

- Developing a negative perception of books or texts that feature a variety of Englishes such as African American Vernacular English or Spanglish
- Valuing 'classical' literature as the only "real literature"
- Maintaining a closed-minded attitude toward books in verse, graphic novels, books by authors of color, etc.

Ways to dismantle a worship of the written word in reading instruction:

- Incorporate texts and books that feature various types of formats and various forms of English.
- Consider incorporating visual texts and visual analyses.

The following table lists three examples of texts that challenge this trait and can be used in classrooms (Figure 3). I do recommend you review the texts first before putting them in student hands so you can determine their best use.

Figure 3: Multimodal Texts

TEXT	FORMATS WITHIN THE BOOK
Citizen **(Rankine 2014) Grades 10-12**	Poetry, visual media, prose
The Forgetting Tree **(Paris 2017) Grades 11-12**	Essays, pictures, poems, prose, African American Vernacular English
Puerto Rico Strong **(Newlevant, Rodriguez 2018) Grades 8-12**	Graphic novels, prose, poems, memoir, fiction, nonfiction, Spanglish

Trait: *Only One Right Way*

To understand this trait, consider the historical context of plantations during the period of enslavement in the United States. There was only one way to "succeed." There was only one way to complete tasks. There was only one way to survive. There was only one way to live.

This way was the way of the enslaver.

The phrase "my way or the highway" embodies this ideal. And while we may laugh at a person who says that, we practice this as a society. Schools are a part of this social project. and in They were designed to be a conduit of this society's values, therefore all of these ideas are embedded in the infrastructure. This trait is present in classrooms across the country in some of the following ways:

- Believing that there is one right way to read and consume a text and once students learn that method, they'll use it forever.
- Perceiving students as "problems" when they don't adopt or use the teacher's reading method.
- Expecting students to process texts one way such as annotating, highlighting, or using Post-it's®.
- Creating reading assessments that don't allow for various modes of demonstrating student learning.

A student in this classroom receiving this type of instruction may internalize only-one-right-way thinking in terms of their reading identity. They may exhibit the following reading attitudes:

- Students reading only happens in class or in designated spaces the teacher has identified
- Students do not do independent reading or select books to read by choice. They simply comply with the teacher's reading instructions.

Ways to dismantle the "only one right way" value in reading instruction:

- Allow students freedom of choice when they read and how they process that reading.
- Notice what students do when they read to make sense of what is being read, and consider adopting those methods or offering them to other students as options.
- Keep in mind that you serve students, so learning about them and their ways is crucial to helping them develop as readers.

Trait: *Individualism*

We love to believe in the solitary hero, narrative conquering obstacles are overcome based on their mental fortitude. However, this narrative is unique to the U.S. Compared to many other countries with collectivist cultures, reaching "glory" alone or "the top" alone symbolizes leaving loved ones behind, reflecting a selfish pursuit.

Individualism is that it is underscored by the belief that everyone begins on an equal footing, which is not true. And when some of us from the global majority do start on somewhat of an equal footing with our White counterparts, there are systems and barriers in place to serve as obstacles along the way. This celebration of individualism is present in schools in the following ways:

- Valuing reading and processing one's understanding as a solo activity
- Celebrating individual students who complete books "on their own"
- Ignoring the sociopolitical context of the readers in the room to analyze stances they take when reading, what biases they hold as readers of a specific book, and the historical and political time and place of their reading it
- Reading competitions are valued and celebrated rather than cooperation and reading as a community

- Veiling "independent reading time" as a period for when students complete their work alone, potentially at the expense of community building time or teacher-student rapport-building.

A student in this classroom receiving this type of instruction may internalize a value for individualism in terms of their reading identity. They may exhibit the following reading attitude:

- Believing that reading happens alone and books are read in isolation.

Ways to dismantle individualism in reading instruction:

- Including partner reading and community reading as an important value and method to reading instruction
- Helping students to evaluate and analyze their reader identity and sociopolitical context, including their biases.

Below I've visualized a process (Figure 4) showing how you can include partner and community readings to process a text. Each circle is representative of a step or action students take to read and process in community. One way to implement this process is to facilitate the rounds using a timer. For example, you would time the inner circle to be 10 or 15 minutes and then notify the group it's time to move to the 2nd circle for which they'll have 10 more minutes. Once that time is up, the class returns to a whole-room discussion for 30 minutes or whatever duration you determine. Another idea for implementing this process can be to use a stations approach. For example, station 1 in one corner of the room is for partner work. When students are done, they can move to station 2. This allows you as the facilitator to see where students are needing assistance and meet their needs accordingly. It also invites moment into the reading process and is self-paced.

Figure 4: Collaborative Process

OKAY, NOW BREATHE.

One of the benefits of analyzing the traits of White Supremacy culture is to be able to tackle the ways our practices are unconsciously making it impossible for us and our students to work toward liberation. When we don't do this work, our push for equity or our desires to be antiracist are just that: pushes and desires. They're not change-making actions.

The desires are the foundation to the action. Our motivation is necessary, yes, but it cannot end there. Our desire to bring about change and our heartfelt motivation to do something, alone, aren't enough.

What is potential without execution?

We have tons of potential to bring about change, but without action there is no execution; the status quo stays the same. Being able to name the practices, the details, the "little things" that make the big thing operate is one way to deconstruct it all and dismantle the monster that is racism. This lack of introspective work is at the core of political movements we see today. Some of the laws, specifically one of the ones in Florida (where I now reside) is concerned about white discomfort. Have they ever considered Black discomfort when the n-word is featured in racist books, for example? Have they ever considered Asian discomfort when their voices are excluded from curriculum? Have they considered Indigenous discomfort when their histories are whitewashed and left out?

If this work weren't important and if doing antiracist work weren't a disruption and upsetting the oppressive structures in place, they wouldn't be legislating against it.

We have to start with ourselves.

As educators dedicated to dismantling systemic racism in our practice and field, our journey must move us from the theoretical into the practical. We have uncovered the subtle traits of White Supremacy culture in education. Now, we shift from theory to practice through personal reflection. I want us to bridge the gap between research, theory, and implementation. To guide this process, I am drawing from the powerful work of several academic elders whose work provides us with opportunities to dig deep and take action.

These meticulously chosen quotes in the rest of this workbook, will prompt you to consider new ideas and ways of thinking. Each quote is a stepping stone, inviting you to keep going and pushing. I want you to consider your intersectional identities, experiences, and teaching practices within the context of antiracist pedagogy.

Remember that none of this is passive. Each prompt and each page is a call to action. I want you to embrace the discomfort these questions will inspire and be open to transformation! These prompts are a compass leading us to antiracist change.

I am committed to unearthing bias, dismantling oppression, and establishing loving antiracist classrooms. I want to create a space where students are empowered to bring about necessary change. Are you?

Let's dream a new educational landscape together.

"CULTURALLY SUSTAINING PEDAGOGY EXISTS WHEREVER EDUCATION SUSTAINS THE LIFEWAYS OF COMMUNITIES WHO HAVE BEEN AND CONTINUE TO BE DAMAGED AND ERASED THROUGH SCHOOLING."
— DJANGO PARIS

CULTURALLY SUSTAINING PEDAGOGIES
REFLECTION EXERCISE

BELOW ARE QUOTES FROM DR. DJANGO PARIS AND DR. SAMY Alim's book *Culturally Sustaining Pedagogies*.[5] After the quotes are reflection questions to help us think about application.

> "The purpose of "state-sanctioned" education has been to assimilate students and enact a violent, white-centered ideology." (1)

> "CSP seeks to perpetuate and foster- to sustain- linguistic, literate, and cultural pluralism as part of the schooling for positive social transformation." (1)

> "CSP exists when educators are intentionally sustaining the lifeways of communities who have been historically (and continue to be) oppressed through schooling." (1)

> "There is a fallacy to measuring ourselves/students of color against white middle class norms that dictate success and normalcy." (2)

> "The term relevant (from culturally relevant teaching) does not do enough to explicitly support the goals of maintenance and social critique. It is quite possible to be relevant to something without ensuring its continuing and

5. This book was published by Teachers College Press in 2017. The concept was first published in 2012 in an AERA publication

critical presence in students' repertoire of practice and its presence in our classrooms and communities." (5)6

"For too long we have taught our youth (and our teachers) that Dominant American English (DAE) and other white middle-class normed practices and ways of being are the key to power, while denying the languages and other cultural practices that students of color bring to the classroom. Ironically, this outdated philosophy will not grant our young people access to power; rather, it may increasingly deny them that access." (6)

"Research on ethnic studies show that when students' identities are affirmed in the curriculum there is a direct increase in motivation and engagement with school." (101)

Dr. Tim San Pedro introduces the term and concept of sacred truth space, which "pushes the uncritical boundaries found when theorizing about the goals and outcomes of safe spaces in schools." These classroom spaces are sacred and truth-seeking ones where Indigenous students and other students of color are centered and their "ability to share their realities and experiences that counter/ challenge/correct standard knowledge that leads to painful silencing experiences in schooling." In sacred truth spaces students act vulnerably and safety isn't necessarily the goal. Instead the goals include listening and learning from others. (102-103)

"Culture is not static, nor is it trapped in the past." (112)

---

6. If you're not reading this book, then please know that Dr. Gloria Ladson-Billings is a supporter of CSP. Her work is foundational to their work, she is shown deep respect in this chapter, and she authors a chapter later in the textbook, which is unequivocal fire.

QUESTIONS FOR REFLECTION:

1. How do reading teachers center the White gaze in text selection and reading instruction?

2. What would it look like for you not to align your expectations with White middle-class norms of success?

3. What are some ways to celebrate and honor linguistic diversity and dexterity?

4. How does your reading instruction operate as a site for sustaining the cultural ways of being of communities of the global majority?

5. How can your reading instruction go beyond representation into affirmation of the identities of students of the global majority?

6. How does your reading instruction, through text selection, represent and affirm Indigenous identity?

7. How can your reading instruction be a sacred truth space?

8. In light of all this, what is your purpose in teaching?

"I INVITE YOU TO JOIN ME IN RE-VISIONING RESEARCH IN OUR COMMUNITIES NOT ONLY TO RECOGNIZE THE NEED TO DOCUMENT THE EFFECTS OF OPPRESSION ON OUR COMMUNITIES BUT ALSO TO CONSIDER THE LONG-TERM REPERCUSSIONS OF THINKING OF OURSELVES AS BROKEN."
— EVE TUCK

"SUSPENDING DAMAGE"
REFLECTION EXERCISE

"SUSPENDING DAMAGE: A LETTER TO COMMUNITIES" WAS A letter[7] Dr. Eve Tuck wrote to Native communities and communities of color about their troubled relationships with researchers. In this letter, Dr. Tuck addresses the historical patterns and challenges in research, particularly in relation to Native communities. The excerpts provided offer valuable perspectives for our consideration in the context of reading instruction.

Dr. Tuck highlights the issues arising from historical exploitation and the tendency to depict communities as defeated and broken. She challenges the reliance on damage-centered research frameworks, emphasizing the importance of desire-based frameworks that seek to understand complexity, contraction, and the self-determination of lived lives.

Below are excerpts and important points that I think we can consider when it comes to reading instruction. They will move us to reimagine what points of view we use to select texts. This can be a small, yet powerful shift that would increase engagement and a sense of belonging for students of the global majority.

> **"The trouble comes from the historical exploitation and mistreatment of people and material. It also comes from feelings of being over researched yet, ironically, made invisible."**

---

7. Written in 2009, it was published in Harvard Educational Review. It's available for free online.

"For many of us, the research on our communities has historically been damage centered, intent on portraying our neighborhoods and tribes as defeated and broken."

"I believe that for many well-meaning people, it is actually a de facto reliance on a potentially problematic theory of change that leads to damage-centered research. In a damage-centered framework, pain and loss are documented in order to obtain particular political or material gains."

"As I will explore, desire-based research frameworks are concerned with understanding complexity, contradiction, and the self-determination of lived lives.

"Considering the excerpt from Craig Gingrich-Philbrook (2005), desire- based frameworks defy the lure to serve as 'advertisements for power' by documenting not only the painful elements of social realities but also the wisdom and hope. Such an axiology is intent on depathologizing the experiences of dispossessed and disenfranchised communities so that people are seen as more than broken and conquered. This is to say that even when communities are broken and conquered, they are so much more than that—so much more that this incomplete story is an act of aggression."

"It is certainly not a call for another 'd' word: denial. It is not a call to paint everything as peachy, as fine, as over."

QUESTIONS FOR REFLECTION:

1. In what ways can your reading instruction help students develop a more complex understanding of communities of the global majority?

2. What books and what reflection exercises can we assemble for students so that they can explore a more complete story of resilience and joy as it relates to communities of the global majority?

3. In our efforts to promote and inspire empathy in students, how may we have pushed for a damage-centered narrative through our text selections?

4. In what ways have you/can you address how literature has historically portrayed people of the global majority and their communities as defeated and broken?

"CIVILIZED"
LANGUAGE
CAN DEBASE
HUMANS.
— TONI MORRISON

PLAYING IN THE DARK
REFLECTION EXERCISE

AS A NOBEL PRIZE WINNER IN LITERATURE, TONI MORRISON, offers us a valuable lens for re-examining race, racism, and Whiteness in literature. In this section, we will dive into two central concepts: the presence of racial silence in literature and the impact of race and racism on the racist individual. Morrison also named the concept 'White gaze',[8] referenced in this section, which explains the idea of seeing the world through the lens, understanding, and point of view of White people. This idea matters to us in the literature field.

The publication, *Playing in the Dark: Whiteness and the Literary Imagination*[9] is a gift to us for rethinking and engaging in this conversation. As you reflect on Morrison's profound insights, consider the historical dominance of silence and evasion in literary discourse on matters of race. Reflect on how assumptions shaped by White American writers may have marginalized the impact of black people in literature.

Now, let's engage in reflective questioning to unpack the implications of these ideas for our reading instruction.

There seems to be an understanding among people in the literary field that as a result of American literature being written by white males through their genius, those

---

8. Check out the video on YouTube where she talks about this. It's an interview with Charlie Rose. Fire!
9. This book was published in 1992 by Vintage Books and it's still relevant!

views and that genius is removed from Black people in the United States. This Black presence is the core to truly understanding our national literature and voice. It cannot hover at the margins of our literary imagination. (5)

Our national literature has a series of characteristics: individualism, masculinity, social engagement versus historical isolation; critical and dubious moral complexities; the theme of innocence alongside an obsession with death and hell. I have wondered if these are not responses to the Black "Africanist presence." (5)

When this nation was forming, it required nebulous, coded language and specific restrictions to handle the racist constructions and moral weakness at its heart.

Similarly, literature reproduced that coded language and through omissions, contradictions, tensions, and characterizations, the reader can observe a fabricated Black presence at the core of American identity. It is obvious. (6)

When it comes to race, silence and avoidance have always ruled literary conversation. (9)

When I first became a reader I concluded that Black people meant very little or close to nothing in the imagination of white American writers. I believed this because Black characters had such a minimal impact on the plot, other characters, and therefore also the writer's imagination. (15)

QUESTIONS FOR REFLECTION:

1. How has your text selection and curricula maintained the silence and avoidance of Blackness, Indigeneity, and other marginalized groups in literature?

2. Would you agree that the characteristics listed in the quote above (individualism, masculinity, social engagement versus historical isolation; acute and ambiguous moral problematics; the thematics of innocence coupled with an obsession with figurations of death and hell) are aspects of U.S. national literature? If so, how do they relate to or reflect traits of White Supremacy?

3. Have matters of race, silence, and evasion historically ruled literary discourse in your classes? If so, how do you plan to change that? If not, how can you go deeper?

4. How might your instruction have led students to believe that Black people have had little impact on the imagination, or been absent from the imagination, of White American authors?

"YES, AND THE
BODY HAS MEMORY.
THE PHYSICAL
CARRIAGE HAULS
MORE THAN
ITS WEIGHT."
— CLAUDIA RANKINE

CITIZEN
REFLECTION EXERCISE

IN *CITIZEN: AN AMERICAN LYRIC,*[10] A COLLECTION OF POETRY
and criticism, Rankine offers profound insights into the complexities of race and identity in America. Each poem serves as a lens
through which we can examine and interrogate our ideas about
race and other isms. The book, however, is also a journey through
multimedia where Rankine skillfully displays what it feels like to be
hypervisible as a Black person in the United States.

There is one piece, specifically, that I want to use to think about
anti-racist reading instruction. Famous author Zora Neale Hurston
wrote an essay, "How It Feels to Be Colored Me" and Rankine included a visual photographic display of a powerful line in that essay. This photographic visual prompts us to actively contemplate
our practice(s) and should encourage us to explore the impact of
our choices and methods. As we engage with this work by Rakine, I
invite you to delve into thoughtful reflection, pushing aside shame
or guilt, and moving into new actions.

---

10. This was published in 2014 by Graywolf Press. If you don't have it,
    I suggest you get it. The entire book is a powerful experience.

Glenn Ligon
Untitled (Four Etchings) (detail), 1992
Suite of four; softground etching, aquatint, spit bite, and sugarlift on paper
Each 25 x 17.38 inches (63.5 x 44.15 cm)
Edition of 45 and 10 APs
© Glenn Ligon; Courtesy of the artist, Hauser & Wirth, New York, Regen Projects, Los Angeles,
Thomas Dane Gallery, London, and Galerie Chantal Crousel, Paris.

QUESTIONS FOR REFLECTION:

1. How might your curriculum create a white background where your students of the global majority feel "most colored"?

2. How might our books and text selections "throw" students against a "sharp" white background? What makes that white background "sharp"?

"AN ANTIRACIST IDEA IS ANY IDEA THAT SUGGESTS THE RACIAL GROUPS ARE EQUALS IN ALL THEIR APPARENT DIFFERENCES— THAT THERE IS NOTHING RIGHT OR WRONG WITH ANY RACIAL GROUP."
— IBRAM KENDI

HOW TO BE
AN ANTIRACIST
REFLECTION EXERCISE

AWARD-WINNING AUTHOR IBRAM KENDI, PUBLISHED *HOW TO* *Be An Antiracist*[11] and in it he outlines racist and antiracist ideology. Kendi guides us through a nuanced understanding of the forces at play in shaping our perspectives. As we navigate the excerpts I've selected from his book, I welcome you to reflect on how this might connect to your educational experience in the past and your practice today.

The main concept we will explore are assimilationist and segregationist ideas. The quotes below will help you to understand what he means and the following prompts will help you apply the ideas to your approach.

> Racist ideas can be ones that push forth assimilationist ideas. Such an ideology places a racial group as superior to another group and measures them against those standards. Assimilationists typically position white people as superior. (29)

> There is a duel within racist thinking. This is assimilationist ideas clashing with segregationist ideas. Assimilationists believe that people of color can become 'human' just like

---

11. This book was published in 2019 by One World Press. It became famous in 2020 right after George Floyd was murdered and the "White awakening" happened. Fair critique has been made about the concepts in this book, which I share. I do not openly endorse this book, yet I thought this was a salient idea to incorporate.

white people which segregationists don't. They believe the differences are inherent and unchanging. (31)

Ideas that are antiracist are based on the truth that people are equal while different. Assimilationist ideas are rooted in superiority and inferiority, while segregationist ideas surge from a genetics-based argument for a fixed racial hierarchy. (31)

In the United States, white people have advocated for both assimilationist and segregationist policies, while people of color have typically advocated for antiracist policies and sometimes assimilationist ones. (31)

QUESTIONS FOR REFLECTION:

1. How might our curriculum and text selection further assimilationist or segregationist ideology?

2. How might our expectations of success be rooted in assimilationist ideology?

3. What could conquering the "assimilationist consciousness" and the "segregationist consciousness" look like in reading instruction?

ANTIRACIST READING INSTRUCTION STRATEGIES & TIPS

HOW WE ENACT AN ANTI-RACIST READING PEDAGOGY IS nuanced and challenging. Many aspects of our teaching are contextual and based on the students sitting in front of us. Our identity in those spaces influences what we can and want to do. The community we teach in shapes our curricular and pedagogical choices,[12] and these factors are only the tip of the proverbial iceberg.

While the following strategies are sure to inspire ideas and new approaches, I also want to communicate that collaboration is probably the best way to assess, revise, and workshop what we do for an antiracist outcome. Instead of thinking we are individual teachers, we must see ourselves as part of a body and that organism requires collaboration and connectedness in order to succeed.

Additionally, the strategies outlined below are only some of the many options you have. I've focused on four to make this manageable, but also because I think many other tips and ideas fall into these four strategies. Remember that you are not alone. You'll find many educators around the nation practicing robust antiracist strategies, effectively changing students' minds.

---

12. Shameless plug, but I expand on this even further in the first chapter of my second book, *Textured Teaching* (2021).

Pause & Discuss

Given that individuality/isolation and quantity over quality are traits of White Supremacy culture, disrupting those patterns within the classroom is good work. Therefore, stopping in the midst of reading to pause, gather ourselves, and discuss is both good teaching practice, and anti-racist *if* you are intentional.

I want to emphasize that the sense of urgency is also disrupted when we pause and discuss; breaking the rhythm (in strategic ways) to focus on race(ism). When you pause, you want to intentionally build students' consciousness and critical thinking about what they're reading, what is missing, and what they need to draw out. Here are some questions that can guide that discussion:

- What voices are pervasive in this text and why do you think that is?
- Does that voice represent dominant ideals in our culture?
- What perspective is missing and how is it impacting the plot? The characters? The conflict?
- How do issues of race, ethnicity, and identity directly and indirectly present themselves in this text?
- How are people of the global majority treated in this text? If absent, what might that suggest about the text and the author?

Focus On Minor Characters

Often, in novels, (especially the "classics") minor characters are people of the global majority and other marginalized identities. Unfortunately, they are rarely the protagonists, and instead exist as minor characters playing marginal roles. In such cases, granting them some curriculum time is crucial to helping students value these characters, understand their role, and make observations about their presence. Here are some tips for constructing these activities:

Consider a minor character that heavily impacts plot, the protagonist, or the conflict but is overlooked.	Spend a day discussing their role in the plot and consider the story without them. Discussion questions: • How does the plot change when they're missing? • What value does this character bring to the story? • How might that reflect the author's beliefs?
After defining 'racial token', help students consider a minor character that is tokenized.	Discussion questions: • How are these characters tokenized to serve the White characters? • How do these tokenized characters support a White gaze (Morrison)? • Explore with students what this character could do to break out of this tokenized role. Imagine how that might change the plot and other characters.
Consider a minor character that employs a stereotype.	Discuss the stereotype that the character is performing and how that serves the other characters in the story. Discussion questions: • Does the stereotype support white Supremacist ideas? • Does it maintain a racist status quo? • How does this stereotype allow other characters to get away with particular behaviors or choices? • How does this stereotype, and its presentation in the text, communicate the values of the author/writer?

Build a Counternarrative

One way to have intentional and explicit anti-racist conversations is by building a counternarrative with and for students. A counternarrative, or counter storytelling, is one of the tenets of critical race theory.[13] Through a counternarrative we are gain a point of view from the marginalized that counters, with depth, the dominant narrative told about them. These counternarratives are nuanced and truthful, going beyond stereotypical portrayals often created by non-community members. The texts and materials selected for your curriculum should predominantly be written from the perspective of community members whose stories are being told. A counternarrative can offer a healthy and holistic understanding of groups of people.

Teaching counternarratives can actually be an achievable exercise, that with practice, can lead to powerful learning. This can be accomplished by identifying the stereotypes held against certain groups, and creating units of study that deliberately offer alternate views. For example, there exists a stereotype about Black men as animalistic, barbaric, and violent.[14] Building a counternarrative could include creating a text set where Black men are protagonists, involved in tender, honest, and loving relationships of all kinds. It would require showing Black men as gentle fathers, loving husbands, emotional brothers, dependable friends, queer people, and more.

To initiate the unit, have an explicit conversation about the stereotype, built on the foundation of rapport with students and establishing discussion norms. These are not intellectual-only conversations; they rightly include heart-talk. If necessary, define "stereotype," and discuss collectively what some of those stereotypes

---

13. Yes, that monster. One of the versions is available for free as a PDF. It's called Critical Race Theory: An Introduction by Delgado and Stefancic.

14. Simply Google "black men as violent stereotype" and you'll see. There were too many resources to cite one.

might be based on what they have heard, have been told, or have seen. This conversation necessitates an understanding that these are hurtful and harmful ideas, demanding a level of sobriety for the discussion. It should not elicit laughter or jokes, since Black men continue to die due to the ingrained stereotypes (and more) placed upon them.

Next, you'd introduce the texts the class will be engaging in as a more holistic understanding of Black men. During and after the reading, it's important to point students to the antiracist counter storytelling the texts are conveying, in addition to the literary work we teach in class. In the chart that follows I've included two text set examples that speak to two different racial stereotypes (Figure 5). My hope is that you can see how a diverse range of texts can offer students a holistic perspective.

Figure 5: Counternarrative Text Sets

RACIAL STEREOTYPE	TEXTS FOR A COUNTERNARRATIVE
Black men as animalistic and violent	**Books:** *Heavy* (Laymon), *Ghost* (Reynolds), *Blue Ink Tears* (Germán) **Television and Film:** Doc McStuffins, *Moonlight* **R & B singers:** Babyface, Tevin Campbell, Boyz II Men
Latinas as sexy and fierce	**Books:** *Furia* (Mendez), *The Poet X* (Acevedo), *Borderless* (de León), *Gabi, A Girl in Pieces* (Quintero), *Olga Dies Dreaming* (Gonzalez), *Juliet Takes a Breath* (Rivera) **Television and Film:** *Real Women Have Curves* film, Dolores Huerta (documentary)

Teaching Sociopolitical Context

I can't emphasize this strategy enough. This approach involves guiding students to perceive the word in the midst of the world and their role in that dynamic interaction. It is indispensable because it enables students to understand the impact of their identity on their comprehension and analysis. It allows them to understand how reading and writing do not occur in an isolated manner, but they are communal, both physically and socially. When I was in graduate school, one of my dear professors, Dr. David Kirkland, introduced a concept for analyzing a text within a sociopolitical context. He spoke about looking within, around, and against a text. See the following image (Figure 6) for a visual articulation.

Reading within a text involves seeking meaning and making sense of the content, encompassing basic reading comprehension and text-dependent literary analysis. Reading around a book entails considering the sociopolitical context in which it was written, assessing the factors that influenced the author during the writing and publication. Reading against a text involves critiquing, evalu-

Figure 6: Critical Reading of Texts

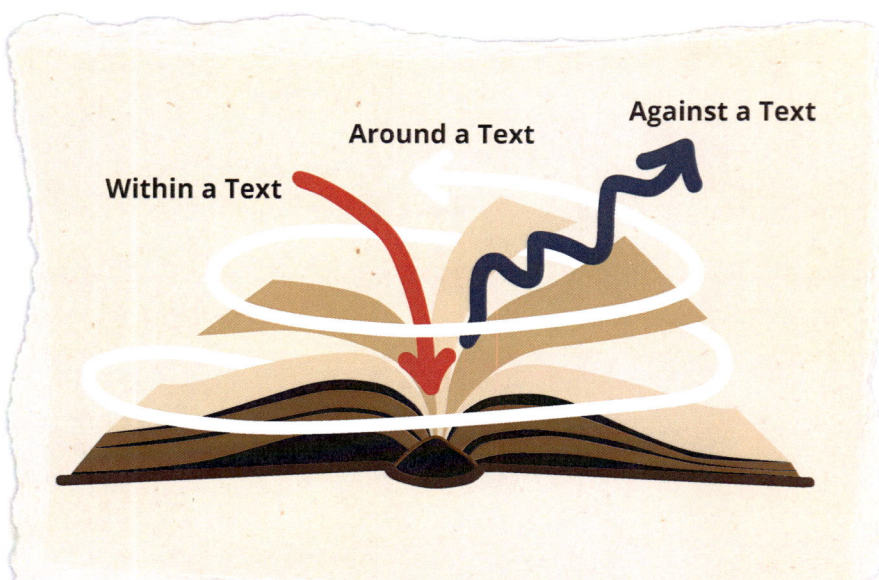

Against a Text

Around a Text

Within a Text

ating, and questioning it, refusing to unquestionably accept what the author presents but believing that the publication invites study and interpretation. Of course, it is especially important to do this work of going against a text with books that are deemed "classics" and literary giants.

I recommend initiating the exploration by having students explore their own identity and positionality. Following that, encourage them to engage in dialogue where they extend their focus beyond themselves. Here are some questions to guide that conversation with students:

- What impact does our current political context have on my interpretation of this text?
- Why does the time period when this text was written matter to me as a reader?
- How does the author's racial identity impact the content?
- How does my racial and ethnic identity impact my reading and interpretation of this text?
- How might popular culture impact my analysis of this text, what I notice and don't notice?
- Is there any trace of colonialism in this text and how might that be related to the author's identity?

Encourage probing questions about social class, partisan ideas, sexuality, and gender as well. Disrupting the silence around these topics is key to establishing a classroom space that is open and honest. The objective of this exercise and ensuing discussions is for students to see themselves in new ways.

For students of the global majority, this allows them to place themselves in broader social conversations and equips them language to articulate their perspectives. In the case of White students, it aids them in shattering the barrier of silence and avoidance, compelling introspection. The result is an awareness that will, hopefully, lead them to a better understanding of the world.

ADDITIONAL RESOURCES

THANK YOU FOR READING.

I want to invite you to take some next steps to support this work:

- Leave a review of this book on Amazon.
- Participate in the book's corresponding course on our website.

https://rb.gy/6yn3qw

- Talk to a colleague or others and form a study group to read and discuss this book together.
- Welcome me to work with you and your colleagues/team. Together, we can reach more people and do this work.